A BLACKFOOT LEGEND

◆◆BUFFALO DANCE◆◆

RETOLD BY

NANCY VAN LAAN

ILLUSTRATED BY

BEATRIZ VIDAL

LITTLE, BROWN AND COMPANY

Boston New York Toronto London

GLOSSARY

Wo-ka-hit!	Listen!
Ah-sa-ke-wah!	I don't care!
Ni-tun!	My daughter!
Ma-me-at-si-kim-i	[Precise translation unclear but probably] Bird of magical powers
Ni-nah-ah!	My father!

SOURCES

Campbell, Joseph. *The Masks of God: Primitive Mythology.* New York: Viking, 1959.
Ewers, John. *The Blackfeet.* Norman, Oklahoma: University of Oklahoma Press, 1958.
Grinnell, George Bird. *Blackfoot Lodge Tales.* Lincoln, Nebraska: University of Nebraska Press, 1962.
Haines, Francis. *The Buffalo.* New York: Thomas Y. Crowell Co., 1970.

Text copyright © 1993 by Nancy Van Laan
Illustrations copyright © 1993 by Beatriz Vidal

First Edition

Library of Congress Cataloging-in-Publication Data

Van Laan, Nancy.
  Buffalo dance : a Blackfoot legend / retold by Nancy Van Laan; paintings by Beatriz Vidal. — 1st ed.
    p.   cm.
  Summary: A retelling of the Blackfoot legend about the ritual performed before the buffalo hunt.
  ISBN 0-316-89728-0
  1. Siksika Indians — Legends. [1. Siksika Indians — Legends. 2. Indians of North America — Legends.]
I. Vidal, Beatriz, ill. II. Title.
E99.S54V36   1993
398.24′5297358 — dc20   92-15444

10 9 8 7 6 5 4 3 2

NIL

Published simultaneously in Canada by Little, Brown & Company (Canada) Limited
Printed in Italy

For Bill Whip-poor-will Thompson,
a wise elder and dear friend who knows the ways of
all those who live on Earth, our mother
N.V.L.

To the memory of my beloved Teacher, Ilonka Karasz,
and of Joseph Campbell, whose ideas kindle my quest
B.V.

INTRODUCTION

Long ago, when the Blackfoot Indians roamed the hills of the Great Plains of Montana, they depended on the meat and fur of the buffalo to survive. These animals, which weigh over a ton apiece and grow to be six feet tall, were not easy to hunt. So the Blackfeet set up elaborate traps called *piskuns* to overtake them. Large boulders and brush were placed in the shape of a V at the edge of a cliff. When the buffalo drew near, the hunters would jump out from behind the boulders and surprise them, causing these mighty beasts to stampede and fall off the cliff into the trap.

Before and after each hunt, certain men of the tribe were chosen to perform a ritual called the buffalo dance. This ceremony was a special way to thank the buffalo for sacrificing some of their own so that the Blackfoot tribe could survive. The dance was also a way of showing the buffalo respect, something that white men, whose careless killing caused the buffalo's near-extinction, never did.

The story that follows tells how the buffalo dance came to be and why it is one of the most sacred rituals of the Blackfoot people.

There was once a time long ago when the buffalo, though plentiful, could not be caught. The large *piskun* that the Blackfoot village had built to trap them was useless. No buffalo would go near the cliff's edge. With winter on its way, the whole village would starve unless meat was found soon.

Early one morning, a young Blackfoot woman woke up. Her family was still sleeping soundly. Silently, she crept out of the tipi. All was quiet. There was nothing to eat, but she gathered a few roots and twigs to make tea. Then she carried some skin bags down to the far stream to fetch water. The stream was laced with ice, and the air was so cold and sharp that she could see her breath.

EARLY MORNING   WOMAN WALKS TO STREAM

Shhh! What was that?

A faint crunching sound caused the young woman to stand up and listen. What could it be?

She looked up at the jagged rocks and boulders where her people had built the *piskun*.

Buffalo! Hundreds of them grazing, unaware that she was there. And they were right on the edge of the cliff!

"*Hai-yah!*" she cried. "Please, please, jump into the *piskun!*" The buffalo did not look up.

Again she pleaded, but the buffalo turned their backs and kept on eating.

Oh, how hungry her people were, but what could she do? If she returned to her village for help, the buffalo might vanish. Desperately, she cried out, "I promise to marry one of you if only you will jump!" How could she say such a thing? She did not mean it.

There was a brilliant flash of light, then thunder. The ground trembled. Hundreds of buffalo began drawing nearer and nearer to the *piskun*. The young woman held her breath.

WOMAN SEES BUFFALO

Suddenly, the mighty buffalo were stampeding, running this way and that. She saw one jump, then another, until soon many buffalo were jumping, tumbling, and falling off the cliff. She was afraid — so afraid that her arms and legs lost all feeling.

Just then, a whir of black-and-white feathers darted about, encircling the young woman. The magpie sounded warning: *"Tri-li-li-li-li-li!"* But it was too late. The young woman had already made her promise. And the buffalo had already jumped.

Most of the buffalo had jumped to their deaths, but a few, including the largest and fiercest bull, had survived the fall. The bull snorted and stomped his feet, then leapt over the *piskun* walls and came toward the young woman.

MAGICAL BIRD COMES

"Come," the huge buffalo said, taking hold of her arm.

"No!" the young woman cried. "No!" Twisting and turning, she broke free, then started to run off.

"Don't leave!" the buffalo called. "You must keep your promise. You must stay with me forever. See how full the *piskun* is? I am their chief. You must honor your words."

The young woman looked over at the *piskun*. It was full — full of buffalo who had died because of what she had promised! Her people would now have plenty of meat and furs for the winter. She must do as he said. So she sadly followed the buffalo chief over the bluff and out to the prairie.

DEAD BUFFALO   PRISONER

When the young woman did not return to her village, the Blackfoot people worried. Something had caused the young woman to disappear, but what?

Then they saw the *piskun* full of buffalo.

"*Wo-ka-hit! Wo-ka-hit!*" cried the father of the young woman. "She is with them!"

But searching among the bodies of the great beasts, the villagers could find no trace of the man's daughter. It was as though she had vanished like the warmth of the prairie wind.

The tribe knew that there was no time to search for her, for there was much work to be done.

"*Ah-sa-ke-wah! Ni-tun!*" The father missed his young daughter too much to care about food or warm furs.

So while the meat was divided equally among the tribe and the great skins were stretched to dry, the man went off to find his daughter.

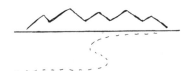

ABUNDANCE OF BUFFALO   MAN GOES TO MOUNTAINS

The father searched until the sun was no longer up in the sky. But he found no daughter, no buffalo — nothing but the frost that covered the rolling hills and the barren trees that offered no food to eat. He lay down to rest near a wallow, a place of shallow water and tall grass.

Suddenly, a beautiful bird with black-and-white feathers fluttered out of the darkness and alit on his shoulder. The man cried out in surprise. *"Ha! Ma-me-at-si-kim-i!* You are said to have strange powers. Perhaps you can help me."

Speaking softly, the man told the bird how he was searching for his daughter. "If you see her, tell her that I am waiting by the wallow."

EVENING   MAGICAL BIRD COMES

Of course the magpie knew exactly where the young woman was, for this was the same bird who had tried to warn her. So he flew directly over to the herd of buffalo, who were sleeping soundly, and pecked the young woman lightly on the cheek.

"Shhh! Shhh!" the young woman whispered, for the buffalo chief was asleep beside her. "Go back and tell my father to wait."

For hours she had been lying on the cold, rough earth, too frightened to sleep. But knowing that her father was nearby made her even more fearful. She was afraid that he would be killed. Somehow she must go to him, to explain and to warn him away.

BIRD SPEAKS TO WOMAN

Luckily, soon after the magpie departed, the great bull woke up and told the young woman to get water, for he was thirsty.

Oh, how gladly she would do as he asked! The young woman took a horn from the bull's head and hurried through the darkness to the wallow. When she saw her father sitting there, she cried out, "Father, go at once or you will be killed!"

"You are my daughter," he answered. "I have come to take you home."

"No! No!" she cried. "In exchange for food for our people, I have promised to stay here forever. I must bring this water to the buffalo chief. You must go back to our village without me."

Quickly, she returned to the bull.

NIGHT

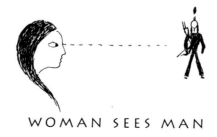

WOMAN SEES MAN

But immediately, the buffalo chief knew something was wrong. He sniffed the air, then snorted. "Ha! A man is closeby!"

"Oh, no, there is no one," the young woman said. Then she pointed as the brave magpie darted between them. "Look! It is just a harmless bird. Go back to sleep."

The bull's eyes darkened with rage, and the young woman knew that he did not believe her.

"*BU-U-U! M-M-AH-OO!*"

Oh, what a fearful sound that was!

All the buffalo rose up, raised their short tails and shook them, tossed their great heads, and bellowed back.

"*BU-U-U! M-M-AH-OO!*"

They stood for a moment, pawing the dirt. Then the entire herd rushed to the wallow, where they found the young woman's father hidden in the tall grass. They trampled him with their sharp hooves until there was nothing left.

WAR   MAN LIES DEAD

"Oh! Ah! *Ni-nah-ah!* Oh! Ah! *Ni-nah-ah!*" wailed the young woman.

"Ah!" said the bull. "Now, perhaps you see how it is with the buffalo. We, too, have seen our fathers killed — by your people."

The young woman pounded the ground with her fists and wept. The buffalo chief could not help but pity her. He also knew that humans often possessed strange magic, so he said, "This is what I will do for you. If you can bring your father back to life, both of you may return to your people."

So the young woman, bewildered by the task set before her, appealed to the magpie for help. "Please go look in the trampled mud," she said. "Find a piece of my father's body, and bring it to me."

Immediately, the magpie began to tear up the earth with his sharp beak. Pulling hard, he brought up a piece of backbone and flew with it to the young woman.

Tenderly, she placed the bone on the ground and covered it with her robe, then sang:

> Awake! Awake! *Ni-nah-ah!*
> Make yourself whole!

When she removed the robe, there lay her father's body as if dead. Once more, she covered it with the robe and sang:

> O Great Spirit, bring the winds!
> Let them flow through my father
> And awaken his soul.

WOMAN CRIES   MAGIC   WOMAN MAKES MEDICINE

When the young woman took away the robe, her father was breathing. Then he stood up!

"Oh, *Ni-nah-ah!*" the young woman cried. "You are alive!"

The buffalo snorted and pawed the ground, astonished that such a thing could happen. The magpie flew around and around, making a joyful noise. "*Tre-tre-lyah-li-li!*"

"Your medicine is very strong," said the buffalo chief. "Much stronger than ours." He nuzzled the robe as though to better understand its curious magic.

The young woman was so grateful she and her father had been spared that she offered the robe to the buffalo chief. Carefully, she draped it over his massive shoulders. The chief was touched by her kindness. "In turn, we will teach you our dance," he said. "When your people kill our kind, have them do this dance and sing our song. That way, we will come back to life, just as your father has done."

Slowly they began to dance the buffalo dance. Their hooves, pounding the earth in a steady, rhythmic beat, echoed across the prairie like a thousand drums. They bellowed the words to an ancient song, taught to them by the wind. Shaking their shaggy heads like rattles, the buffalo circled around the young woman and her father.

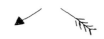

MAGIC   UNION   PEACE

When the dance was over, the buffalo chief said, "Be sure to have your men dress like us for the dance. Let each of them wear a bull's head and a buffalo-skin robe. When we see that your people dance, dressed like us, and hear them sing our powerful song, then we will die willingly, knowing that this ceremony will bring us back to life again. Go now to your home and do not forget what you have seen."

So the father and young daughter returned to their village, and the magpie flew back to his nest of sticks in a thick tangle of bushes by the stream.

At once a great celebration took place and an important council of the chiefs was held. From this day forth, the council decided, young men would be chosen to perform the sacred buffalo dance and sing the sacred song. So that is how it was done before and after each killing of the buffalo.

COUNCIL

And the brave act of this young woman whose name we do not know became legend.
Her story has been handed down for generations through the elders of the Blackfoot tribe.